HERMA

Moby Dick

Adapted by H.Q. Mitchell

mm publications

Introduction

Herman Melville was born in New York in 1819. His father, a merchant, died when Herman was twelve years old leaving his family penniless because he had invested all his money in unsuccessful businesses. Herman had to support himself financially so he got a job as a cabin boy on a New York ship travelling to Liverpool. This was his first job at sea. In later years Herman worked on whalers, taking short breaks from these trips to live among the native people of various Pacific islands.

His experiences from his voyages, as well as the life among the natives, are described in his books *Typee, Omoo, White-Jacket* and of course, *Moby Dick*. The first three books gained Melville great popularity as an author, but they never gave him enough money to live on.

Melville married Elizabeth Shaw in 1847 and had four children with her, however, his marriage was not always a happy one. From 1850 the family lived in Arrowhead, a farm house they bought in Massachusetts, which was very close to Nathaniel Hawthorne's house in Lenox. The two writers became very good friends; so good that, when Melville finished *Moby Dick*, he dedicated it to Hawthorne.

Moby Dick is Melville's most famous and longest work and it is considered one of the masterpieces of American and world literature. However, the book was only recognised as such after the 1920s. When it was first published, it was the major reason for Melville to lose his popularity and never gain it again during his lifetime.

The book tells the adventures of the young sailor Ishmael who goes on a whaling trip with the ship *Pequod*, which is captained by the infamous Captain Ahab.

Two events seem to have inspired Melville's work: the sinking of the Essex, a Nantucket whaleship, by a large sperm whale in 1820, and the killing in the late 1830 of the notorious *Mocha Dick* (*Mocha Dick* was a huge white whale which had often attacked ships violently).

Melville uses symbolism and metaphor to explore major themes such as good and evil, equality, friendship and companionship, obsession and revenge.

The book has a famous opening line – "Call me Ishmael" – and it has inspired many film and television adaptations and even songs. One famous song by the 1970's group Led Zeppelin is named *Moby Dick* because of its length.

Contents

CHAPTER 1

ALL ME ISHMAEL. I AM A SAILOR, AND MY HAPPIEST DAYS HAVE been spent at sea. I have had many exciting adventures in the 'watery part of the world', as I like to call it, but none as thrilling and terrifying as the search for Moby Dick. Yes, I was part of the attempt to kill the cunning white whale and this is my story…

I left Manhattan and arrived in New Bedford, Massachusetts, on a Saturday evening in December, 1851. My plan was to catch a ferry from New Bedford to Nantucket so that I could join the crew of a Nantucket whaling ship. The Nantucket whaling business was a growing industry at that time, with hundreds of ships leaving American shores each year to hunt and kill sperm whales for their oil. The oil, which was extracted from the whale's fat, or blubber, was used for lighting oil lamps and making candles, and was considered particularly valuable. I had always been fascinated by the beauty and greatness of whales; they lived in wild and distant seas, and I knew that whale-hunting would provide me with the opportunity to explore exotic, far-away places.

Unfortunately, I missed the ferry to Nantucket and discovered, to my disappointment, that the next ferry was scheduled to leave on Monday. With only a few cents in my pocket, I was forced to search for some very cheap accommodation. I made my way through the dark, bitterly cold streets of New Bedford, gazing into the candlelit windows of various inns, until I found one that looked affordable. The swinging sign above the door read: *The Spouter-Inn;* the owner's name, Peter Coffin, was painted in white underneath.

I walked into the inn and found it full of sailors who were chatting merrily. After a brief search, I located the landlord and told him I wished to rent a room.

"No rooms left, I'm afraid," said Coffin. "But there is one bed left… would you mind sharing a room with a harpooner?"

I did mind, in fact, I minded very much. But the landlord insisted that the harpooner was a decent fellow, and managed to persuade me that sharing a room with a perfect stranger was a much better option than spending the night out in the cold.

"All right," I said. "I suppose I have no choice."

"Good," said Coffin. "Take a seat in the dining room and I'll bring you some dinner."

I made my way to the dining room and sat down at the table with four or five other sailors. Without delay, Coffin brought us a meal consisting of very generous portions of meat, potatoes and dumplings. The food was absolutely delicious and I quickly devoured every last bite.

"Say, Mr Coffin," I said as the landlord cleared away my plate, "is the harpooner here?"

Coffin chuckled. "No, he won't be back till much later. He's out selling his head."

"His head?" I exclaimed. "What on earth do you mean?"

"The harpooner has just returned from New Zealand, where he collected some human heads," the landlord explained. "He's managed to sell all of them, except one. He has to sell it tonight; it wouldn't be right to try to sell a human head on Sunday morning when people are going to church…"

I could hardly believe my ears. "Mr Coffin, are you mad?" I shouted. "Are you really planning to put me in a room with some savage who's out selling human heads?"

Coffin grinned. "Calm down, young man. The heads are made of wax… I think. I assure you that the harpooner poses no threat to you. Anyway, it's almost midnight and I doubt he'll be returning to the inn tonight. Let me show you to your room; I'm sure you'd like to get some sleep."

Reluctantly, I followed the landlord up the staircase to a small room at the end of a narrow passageway. The room contained a table, chair and two beds. I noticed a bag of clothing on the floor, which I assumed belonged to my room-mate. The landlord wished me good night and I put on my nightwear and went to sleep.

I was awakened an hour or so later by the sound of the door opening. The harpooner had returned. I decided to remain perfectly still and not say a word until my room-mate noticed me. The harpooner was a huge man, holding a candle in one hand and a scarily lifelike head in the other. I watched him as he placed the candle on the floor and opened a large canvas bag from which he removed an axe and a wallet. Then, he put the head in the bag and closed it. The light from the candle was weak and I could only just see his face: his skin appeared to be yellowish-purple in colour and his cheeks were

covered in large black squares which I assumed were tattoos. He was bald except for a few strands of hair which were twisted up on his forehead.

I had never seen a more terrifying-looking man in my life and had he not been standing between me and the door, I would have run out of there as fast as my legs could carry me. The harpooner changed into his nightwear, blew out the candle and climbed into his bed.

My heart was beating so loudly, I could hear it beating in my ears. I decided I couldn't share a room with a madman after all, and I jumped out of bed and ran to the door. Of course, it was pitch black in the room, and I tripped over the harpooner's bag.

The harpooner sat up in surprise. "Who's there?" he shouted.

"Please don't hurt me!" I cried. "Landlord! Mr Coffin! Someone save me, please!"

The landlord heard my screams and burst through the door a moment later, dressed in a nightgown and carrying a lamp.

"Don't be afraid," said the landlord, as he helped me to my feet. "Queequeg won't harm a hair on your head."

"Are you sure about that?" I said.

The landlord laughed. "Queequeg, young Ishmael here will be sharing your room with you tonight, is that all right?"

Queequeg was silent for a moment. "That's fine," he grunted.

"Good," said the landlord. "I'll see you both in the morning. Good night." With that, the landlord walked out of the room and closed the door.

"Don't worry, young man, I won't hurt you," said Queequeg.

I nodded and climbed back into my bed. Feeling strangely reassured, I fell asleep almost immediately.

***

The next morning, Queequeg and I woke up early and made our way to the dining room. I had the opportunity to meet some of the other guests at the inn; they were all whalers: carpenters, blacksmiths and harpooners. Some had only recently returned from a voyage; others were making plans to leave again. We enjoyed a breakfast of coffee and hot rolls, while Queequeg dined on large pieces of steak

which looked barely cooked.

Once we'd eaten, Queequeg lit his pipe and made his way to the lounge room, and I decided to go for a stroll. I returned to the inn after lunch and found the harpooner sitting in front of the fireplace, polishing a small wooden figure. Not wanting to spend the rest of the day by myself, I pulled up a chair and sat down beside him.

"Are we going to share a room again tonight?" asked Queequeg, without looking up.

"Yes," I said.

"In that case, we are brothers," he said, extending a hand to shake mine.

I smiled and shook his hand. We spent the rest of the day talking and getting to know one another better. Queequeg told me that he was a native of the South Pacific island of Rokovoko. His father had been the king of his tribe and Queequeg was next in line to take his place. But young Queequeg wanted adventure, so, one day, he hid on

board a whaling ship that had anchored briefly at his island. Queequeg managed to persuade the angry captain to keep him on board and teach him the business of whaling. In no time at all, Queequeg became an expert harpooner, known for his skill and accuracy.

"I want to see more of the world," he said. "That's why I'm here. I want to go on a whaling trip."

"Really?" I asked with delight. "I am also going to Nantucket to find a whaling ship."

"We'll go together," said Queequeg and smiled broadly. "After all, we are brothers now."

After supper, we returned to our room and Queequeg gave me thirty silver dollars, half his fortune. Of course, I told him I couldn't take it, but he wouldn't listen to me. In his culture, he said, it was customary to share one's belongings with one's family members.

I felt extremely touched by Queequeg's kindness and generosity; it felt good to make a new friend.

CHAPTER 2

On Monday morning, Queequeg and I caught the first ferry to Nantucket. We arrived in the early evening, and rented a room at an inn called *The Try Pots*. After a hearty fish stew supper, we discussed our plan for the next day.

"Yojo says you have to choose a ship for our voyage," Queequeg informed me. He said he had spoken with his idol, Yojo – the small wooden figure he'd been polishing the day before – and that the statue had insisted that I be the one to choose the whaling ship on which we were to travel.

Of course, I did not wish to make this important decision alone, and I tried to convince Queequeg that the idol was wrong, but my new-found friend wouldn't listen to anything.

"But, Queequeg, it's my first time on a whaling ship," I protested. "I know nothing about whaling boats."

"Yojo is always right," declared my friend. "You will choose the right ship."

So, the next morning, I walked to the harbour alone, while Queequeg and Yojo stayed at the inn. After a lot of searching, I discovered that there were three whaling ships that were about to leave for long voyages: the *Devil-dam*, the *Tit-bit*, and the *Pequod*. I inspected all three, and decided that the *Pequod* would be the most suitable.

The ship was about fifty years old and made from a dark brown wood which had faded considerably as a result of years spent under the harsh sun and fierce seas. The sides of the ship were lined with two rows of pointy whale teeth and the tiller had been made out of the jawbone of a whale. At first glance, the ship reminded me of an Ethiopian emperor wearing a necklace of polished ivory.

"Excuse me," I said, addressing myself to an elderly gentleman who was sitting under a covering on the deck. "Are you the captain?"

"Who wants to know?" said the old man.

"My name is Ishmael," I replied. "I want to sign up for the next voyage."

"Do you know anything about whaling?" asked the man.

"Uh, no, sir," I confessed. "But I'm eager to learn. You see, sir, I want to see the world."

The old man sighed. "The whaling business isn't a game, young man. It's to be taken very seriously. And if you don't believe me, ask Captain Ahab."

"Who's Captain Ahab?"

"The captain of this ship."

"Oh," I said. "But I thought you were the captain of this ship, sir."

"No," said the man. "My name is Peleg. I am the co-owner of the *Pequod*; the other owner's name is Bildad. It is our responsibility to hire the crew and make sure that the ship is stocked with all the necessary supplies… Anyway, as I was saying, I suggest you take a look at Captain Ahab before you commit yourself to this voyage; you might think twice about going whaling when you see that the captain has only one leg…"

"What do you mean, sir?" I exclaimed. "Did the captain lose his leg to a whale?"

"He didn't just lose his leg," said Peleg, "the leg was crunched up, chewed up and devoured by the biggest and most terrifying whale you've ever seen! That whale was a monster!" The old man threw his hands up in the air to emphasise the size of the whale, and I took a cautious step back. "Now, young man," Peleg continued, looking at me with his eyes narrowing, "are you sure you still want to go whaling?"

Though Peleg's story was a little alarming, I was more determined than ever to join the crew of the *Pequod*. "Yes, sir," I said. "I still want to go."

The old man raised a curious eyebrow. "Fine, then follow me," he said. Peleg led me to a cabin where I was introduced to his colleague, Bildad. It took just a few minutes to negotiate my salary and sign the necessary paperwork. I told the men that I would return the next day with a very skilled harpooner who would be a great asset to the crew.

As Peleg showed me out of the cabin, I asked him to tell me more about Captain Ahab. "He's a good man, about sixty years old; intelligent and well-educated," said Peleg. "He's very brave

and, some would say, quite mysterious. He's an excellent sailor and certainly the best harpooner I've ever seen. But he can be moody and bad-tempered; which is understandable, given the suffering he's endured. I doubt you'll meet him before the ship sets sail; he hasn't been feeling too well and is at home, resting."

I thanked the man for his time and made my way back to the inn. I was quite curious to meet this Captain Ahab; I found his story to be both sad and exciting. I could hardly wait to tell Queequeg my news.

***

The next day, Queequeg and I returned to the *Pequod*, where the harpooner's salary was determined and the relevant papers were signed. We left the ship in a jolly mood, talking excitedly about the journey that lay ahead, when we suddenly ran into a strange man. He was dressed in a faded jacket and torn trousers, and his face was marked with smallpox scars. "Are you travelling on that ship?" he asked, waving a thick finger at the *Pequod*.

"Yes," I answered. "Why?"

"Have you met the captain yet?"

"No," I replied.

"Ahab is a dangerous man, a dangerous man, I tell you. He's obsessed and his obsession has driven him mad! You shouldn't travel on his ship…"

"Obsessed?" I repeated. "With what?"

"The whale! The whale!" shouted the man.

Queequeg and I exchanged glances. "Look here, sir," I said, "I don't know what you're talking about and, frankly, I don't care either. Please step aside and let us be on our way."

The man shook his head. "Don't say I didn't warn you!" he shouted after us.

Queequeg and I walked on, and the strange man was quickly forgotten.

The *Pequod* was scheduled to set sail on Christmas Day. Queequeg and I woke up at 6 o' clock that morning and rapidly made our way to the harbour. It was still dark, and the ship was almost hidden from

view by streaks of grey fog. As we approached the *Pequod*, I thought I saw five dark figures gathered on the deck. I assumed that they were sailors, but when we boarded the ship, we saw there was no one around except for an old man who was sound asleep.

By sunrise, the *Pequod* was noisy with crew members carrying boxes and unpacking their things. We were later informed that Captain Ahab had boarded the ship the night before and that he planned to remain in his cabin. Finally, the anchor was pulled up, and the *Pequod* set off across the icy ocean.

CHAPTER 3

BY THE END OF THE FIRST WEEK AT SEA, I HAD MET MOST OF the members of my crew, including the mates. The mates are the men responsible for captaining the whaleboats, which are lowered into the sea once a whale has been sighted. Each whaleboat crew consists of a mate, a harpooner and four oarsmen.

The chief mate of the *Pequod* was a tall, thin, thirty-year-old man from Nantucket named Starbuck. He was courageous and practical, and was highly respected by the crew. Starbuck chose Queequeg to be his harpooner. The second mate was a friendly, easygoing man named Stubb. When he wasn't catching whales, Stubb spent most of his time puffing on his pipe. His harpooner was an Indian named Tashtego, who had long, dark hair, high cheekbones, and large eyes. The third mate was a short and stout man named Flask. His harpooner was Daggoo, an extremely tall African who wore gold hoop earrings.

Several days passed before Captain Ahab finally made his appearance on the quarterdeck, a section of the ship's upper deck. I was so surprised to see him that I had to pinch myself to make sure I wasn't dreaming. Ahab was a tall, impressive-looking man, and as he stood motionless on the quarterdeck, surveying his sailors below, he reminded me of a solid bronze statue. His hair was streaked with grey, and I noticed a lightning-shaped scar running down the side of his face and neck. Whether he'd been born with that scar, or it was a result of an accident, no one knew for sure. Probably the most striking thing about Ahab's appearance was his false leg, which had been carved out of whalebone. A small hole had been made in the quarterdeck which provided the captain with a place to secure his false leg, thus preventing him from falling over in stormy weather.

Though Ahab's face was set in an empty stare, the deep sorrow in his eyes was obvious. I was suddenly filled with tremendous admiration for him: this was a man who had experienced unimaginable suffering, and yet was determined to continue working as a ship's captain. I felt privileged to be serving under such a brave man.

In the days that followed, I spent most of my time sitting in the crow's nest at the top of the main mast, looking for whales. I must admit that I wasn't exactly the right man for that particular job; the warmth of the sun and the gentle lapping of the waves almost put me to sleep on more than one occasion.

There was very little activity on the ship until, one morning, Ahab ordered the entire crew to assemble on deck. This was a most unusual order and we immediately did as we were told. We arranged ourselves into a neat row, and Ahab walked past us slowly, carefully examining each crew member as he went. Once he'd completed his inspection, he said: "What do you do when you see a whale, men?"

"Call out!" shouted the crew in unison.

"Good!" cried Ahab. "And what do you do next, men?"

"Lower the boats and chase after him!"

Ahab smiled. He was clearly impressed with his crew's enthusiasm. The captain then reached into his pocket and held up a small, shining coin. "Do you see this, men?" he asked. "This is a doubloon, a Spanish gold coin. Starbuck, please get me a hammer."

When Starbuck returned with the hammer, he handed it to Ahab who proceeded to nail the coin to the mast. "Listen carefully, men," said the captain. "Whoever sees the white whale, with its wrinkled brow and crooked jaw; whoever sees him first, will have this coin as a reward!"

The crew cheered, some men even threw their hats in the air, but the three harpooners, Tashtego, Queequeg and Daggoo, remained silent. The captain's description of the whale seemed to trigger distant memories for them.

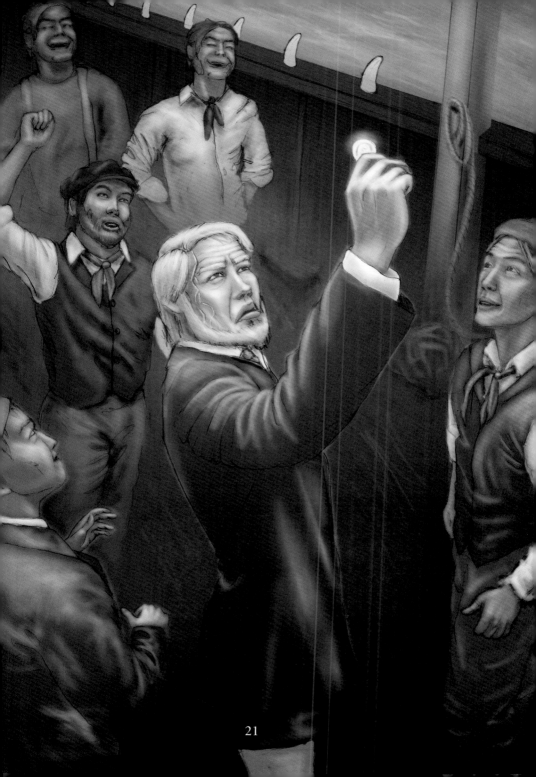

"Sir," said Tashtego, "are you talking about the whale they call Moby Dick?"

"I am," said the captain.

"The strong white whale that moves quickly and escapes all whaleboats?" asked Daggoo.

"Yes…" said the captain.

"The whale that has three harpoons sticking out of him; the one that people say cannot be killed?" asked Queequeg.

"Yes, yes," said the captain impatiently. "The whale you are all describing is Moby Dick."

"Captain Ahab," said Starbuck, "I too have heard of Moby Dick… was he not the whale who took off your leg?"

The captain turned to look at Starbuck, his eyes blazing with anger. "Aye, Starbuck," he hissed, "Moby Dick is the whale who took my leg…" Ahab beat his false leg on the deck and waved his fist in the air. "Moby Dick took my leg!" he roared. "And I will chase him to the ends of the earth; I will hunt him until he sprays black blood and dies! This is why you are all on this ship, to destroy Moby Dick! What do you say, men, can I count on you to help me?"

"Aye, aye!" shouted the crew. "The white whale will die!"

Ahab smiled. "Thank you, my boys," he said. "You will not regret this… Is something wrong, Starbuck? You look troubled."

Starbuck cleared his throat. "Well, sir," he began, "I have no problem killing whales, it is after all our business. But I came here to hunt whales for oil, not for revenge. It makes no sense to me to pursue a dumb animal."

"That 'dumb animal' as you put it, ruined my life," said the captain. "Please, Starbuck," continued Ahab, his tone softening, "the rest of the crew is with me on this and I'd appreciate your support too. Of course, we will kill other whales we may encounter, I understand that my men are here to earn a living… but Moby Dick will remain our priority."

Starbuck was silent for a moment. "How do you plan to track the whale down?"

"I have kept records of all the Moby Dick sightings that have been reported recently," said Ahab. "I've been studying the whale for years; I know his habits and where he hunts for his food. He seems to

appear in the same places at the same time each year, so, with a little luck, we might spot him during the course of our journey."

The first mate sighed. "God help us all," he muttered.

A night of celebration followed the captain's announcement. We ate and danced and listened to stories about Moby Dick until the early hours of the morning. In the days that followed I learned more about how Ahab lost his leg to the whale: during that horrible battle, the whale destroyed Ahab's whaleboats by crashing into them with his broad, flat forehead, and a number of sailors drowned.

In a fit of rage, Ahab, who was in his own whaleboat, attempted to stab the whale with a knife, but the creature burst from the water and tore off the captain's leg with his scissor-sharp teeth. Far from land and medical assistance, the captain spent many days and nights lying in his hammock in terrible pain. It was during that time of suffering that he made up his mind to kill the whale. I felt great sympathy for this courageous man who had been through so much, and decided that I would do what I could to help him.

CHAPTER 4

IT WAS ABOUT A WEEK AFTER THE CELEBRATIONS, ON ONE particularly warm and sunny afternoon, that we finally heard the familiar call that meant a whale was near: "There she blows!" yelled Tashtego from the crow's-nest. We looked up to see the harpooner waving and pointing frantically. "A school of whales, about two miles east!" he shouted.

Chaos broke out on the ship as crew members ran in all directions preparing for the hunt. Once the three whaleboats had been lowered into the water, the harpooners and the oarsmen climbed down rope ladders into the boats, and prepared to take up their positions. Seconds later, we heard the captain's voice on deck. We looked up, and to our great astonishment, saw Ahab with five men dressed in black.

"Those must be the men we saw boarding the ship in Nantucket," I whispered to Queequeg as we climbed into Starbuck's boat.

The harpooner nodded. "They must have been hiding in the hold," he said. "I wonder why they're here."

I noticed the mates exchange confused glances when they heard the captain tell the mysterious men to untie one of the spare boats and lower it into the ocean. The man who was apparently in charge of the group was a tall, dark-skinned Persian, who wore a peculiar turban on his head made from his own braided white hair. His eyes were two dark slits and one tooth poked out from between his thin lips. The man's companions had yellow skin and, I assumed, were probably from the Philippines.

"Ready, Fedallah?" said the captain, turning to address the dark-skinned man.

"Ready sir," said the man.

"Then let's go."

The captain's boat dropped into the ocean and the four whaleboats spread out across the water.

"Spread out! Spread out!" cried Ahab.

"Row, men, row as if your lives depend on it!" yelled Starbuck. We rowed until our arms burned from the effort, but as we approached the whales, they dived into the water and disappeared. Queequeg explained to me that this was called 'sounding' and that whales can 'sound', or stay underwater, for hours at a time. The only hint of the whales' presence was a mass of green and blue bubbles, which an inexperienced whaler could have easily missed.

Suddenly, the whales shot to the surface and began swimming in all directions. The water swirled angrily and we chased after the animals, aware that the high waves could devour us at any moment.

"Get ready, Queequeg!" yelled Starbuck. The harpooner jumped to his feet and sat on the edge of the boat, his harpoon shining in his right hand.

"There's one! That's his hump! Get him, Queequeg!" shouted Starbuck.

As the harpooner prepared to take aim, the boat shook violently; it felt as if we'd been hit by an earthquake. The sail collapsed and I felt the boat break beneath me. The whale Queequeg had been aiming at had smashed into us, and we were all tossed into the water helplessly.

It took about an hour for the *Pequod* to rescue us. We learned later that none of the other boats had had much luck either. Our first attempt to capture a whale had been unsuccessful and, needless to say, the crew was in very low spirits that night. After dinner, the conversation turned to Fedallah and his men.

"Say, Starbuck, what do you think of those strange men the captain brought on board?" asked Stubb.

Starbuck shrugged. "I don't care who he brings with him, as long as they don't get in our way."

Stubb took a puff of his pipe. "Peleg and Bildad probably told the captain not to take part in any whale hunt because of his leg. He obviously decided to bring along his own crew and command his own whaleboat. He's a determined man, that Ahab."

"Aye, that he is," agreed Starbuck.

"I'm not sure I like that Fedallah fellow," said Stubb after a brief pause. "There's something strange about him... There's a rumour going round that he has the ability to see the future... "

Starbuck took a sip of his tea, and said nothing.

Within a few days, the *Pequod* had reached the Cape of Good Hope, at the very tip of Africa. This was a particularly dangerous stretch of water; our ship was hammered by fierce storms and rough waves, and there were moments when I was quite convinced that we would sink. It was thanks to Ahab's impressive leadership that we managed to go past the Cape and enter the calmer waters of the Indian Ocean. We followed a north-easterly course, towards the island of Java.

One morning, Daggoo was sitting in the crow's nest, keeping an eye out for whales, when we heard him shout: "There she blows! There's the white whale!"

Immediately, the four whaleboats were lowered into the ocean, and we rowed like madmen to the spot that Daggoo had indicated. The harpooner had indeed seen something white, but it wasn't Moby Dick. Floating on the water, its long tentacles curling and twisting like deadly snakes, was a giant squid. It was dead.

Starbuck shook his head. "That's a bad omen," he said. "They say that if a whale ship encounters a giant squid, it'll never return home."

We sailed back to the ship in silence. Only Queequeg seemed unconcerned about the squid. "It is a good sign, I think," he whispered to me. "In my experience, when one sees a giant squid, one is very likely to catch a sperm whale soon after."

My wise friend was right. The next day, we spotted an enormous sperm whale swimming just a few metres from the ship, its glossy black back shining in the midday sun. Again, we lowered the boats into the water, and, not wanting to scare the whale off, rowed towards it as quietly as we could.

Stubb's boat was closest to the whale, and he ordered Tashtego to get ready for the kill. The harpooner stood up and took aim, making sure that the harpoon line was securely tied to the boat. The harpoon line is a thin piece of rope which is attached to the harpoon at one end, and the boat at the other. Whales that have been harpooned often attempt to escape; the line connects the whale with the boat, and allows the whalers to continue to pursue the creature if it tries to swim away. It is extremely dangerous to stand in the way of the harpoon line once a harpoon has been thrown; the line becomes as

sharp as a sword and can easily kill a man.

We watched with excitement as Tashtego's harpoon flew through the air and sank into the whale's side; the harpoon line became tense, and the boat was pulled forward for several minutes at high speed as the whale tried to get away. Stubb threw several spears at the animal, until one finally hit the creature's heart. The whale died in a thick pool of its own red blood.

It took all four boats and the strength of thirty-six men to pull the whale back to the *Pequod*. Upon our return, the whale was chained to the side of the ship. The business of extracting the oil would begin the next day.

CHAPTER 5

THE INITIAL PHASE OF FAT REMOVAL IS CALLED 'CUTTING-IN' AND this took place on the morning after the whale had been killed. First, the heavy chains surrounding the whale were tightened and the animal was lifted out of the water. Then, Starbuck and Stubb used long spades to cut a hole in the body, at a point near one of the side-fins, so that a huge hook could be inserted in the animal's flesh.

Attached to the hook was a piece of rope which was tossed over the main mast. Using all their strength, the entire crew pulled on the free end of the rope, until the first strip of blubber had been successfully removed. The whale's body was then made to roll over several times so that the remaining blubber could be peeled off, in much the same way that one would peel the skin off an orange.

The blubber was then cut into strips which were passed below deck through a trapdoor into a room called the blubber-room. Here, the blubber was boiled in large iron pots called try pots, so that the oil could be extracted. Finally, the oil was poured into wooden barrels and the lids were sealed with wax.

Once all the blubber has been removed from a sperm whale, the sailors behead the creature and allow the carcass to float away. The head remains chained to the side of the ship because it contains spermaceti, a valuable wax-like substance used to make candles and lotions. Large sperm whales' heads often contain hundreds of litres of spermaceti, enough to make the crew of any whaling ship very rich indeed.

Extracting the spermaceti from the whale's head was no easy task, and Starbuck chose Tashtego to carry out this challenging task. I watched in awe as the brave harpooner jumped onto the whale's slippery head and began cutting a hole around the spout. Once the hole was large enough, Tashtego used a long spear to cut a hole in the whale's head until he found the area that held the precious spermaceti. After that, a bucket was passed along a rope to the harpooner who lowered it into the whale's head and collected the white, frothy liquid. Tashtego spent at least two hours bent over the head, filling buckets with spermaceti. At around the eightieth or ninetieth bucket, the harpooner stood up, and to the horror of those watching, slipped and fell into the red pulp of the whale's head.

Panic broke out on deck, but the worst was yet to come: Tashtego's efforts to climb out of his prison caused the head to sway and, with a sudden loud crack, the chains broke away from the masts. The ship nearly overturned and many sailors, including me, were knocked off their feet. I held onto the railing and pulled myself up, in time to see the whale's head disappear under the water.

"Tashtego!" I yelled.

"Man overboard!" cried Daggoo.

"I'll get him!" shouted Queequeg. Clutching a sword in his hand, the harpooner rushed to the quarterdeck and dived off. With a mighty splash, my courageous friend Queequeg vanished into the dark blue water. Minutes passed, but there was no sign of either harpooner. Just as I began to fear the worst, Queequeg burst out of the water, pulling Tashtego with him. The crew applauded wildly, and a small boat was lowered to bring the pair back on board.

"How did you manage to save him?" I asked my friend later.

"It was easy," replied Queequeg, "I simply cut a hole in the whale's head and pulled Tashtego out. Remember this lesson, Ishmael: you can achieve just about anything if you have enough faith and courage."

I nodded and smiled.

CHAPTER 6

IN THE TWO WEEKS THAT FOLLOWED, WE WERE FORTUNATE ENOUGH to kill two more whales. But, as we sailed across the Indian Ocean, through the straits of Sunda, and past the islands of Java and Sumatra, whale sightings became less frequent. Though we came across a school of whales at one point, we failed to capture even one.

One sunny afternoon, as Queequeg and I sat on the deck, weaving a mat to pass the time, we noticed a rather foul smell in the air.

"What is that terrible odour?" I said, wrinkling my nose in disgust.

"It smells like something dead," answered the harpooner, raising his head to scan the ocean. "A dead whale, maybe. Though I can't see one floating anywhere near us."

I stood up and, shielding my eyes from the sun's blinding light, examined the shimmering blue water that surrounded us. Suddenly, a dark spot appeared on the horizon. It was a ship.

"Ship ahoy!" I shouted to my fellow sailors.

My announcement caused excitement on deck; life at sea can be very lonely, and sailors are always happy to chat with crews of other ships. But, as the ship drew nearer, accompanied by a group of hungry vultures circling overhead, we realised that it was the source of the horrible smell. Chained to the ship on one side, was a whale that, according to Queequeg, had died of natural causes. "Only a whale that's been dead in the water for a few days can give off such a stink," explained the harpooner.

There was a second whale attached to the other side of the ship, but this one looked dry and wrinkled. I remembered reading once that whales that have died of stomach problems usually shrivel up, and are unlikely to contain much oil.

The ship dropped anchor a short distance from us, and we noticed a French flag flying from the mast. The name *Bouton de Rose* was painted on the side of the ship; it meant 'rosebud'.

"It doesn't smell much like a rosebud," I whispered to Queequeg.

Just then, Stubb, who had been watching the ship with a peculiar smile on his face, turned to us and said: "Men, I need some of you to row out to that ship with me. Those whales could be very useful to us."

"Useful?" exclaimed Queequeg. "I doubt that, Mr Stubb. There isn't enough oil in either of those whales to make even one candle."

"I'm well aware of that, Queequeg," said Stubb. "I'm not interested in oil; I'm interested in other riches…"

I was quite captivated by Stubb's comment and, despite the horrible smell, decided to join him on his mission. Less than ten minutes later, our whaleboat was going up and down alongside the *Bouton de Rose.*

"Hello there!" shouted Stubb. "Do any of you rosebuds speak English?"

One of the crew members stepped forward and looked at us curiously. "I do," he said. "I'm the first mate, and the only one on board who speaks English."

"Excellent," said Stubb. "I hope you don't mind me telling you your business, sir, but those whales of yours won't bring in much oil."

"I know that," said the man with a heavy sigh, "but my captain doesn't. We found these whales floating in the water, and he insisted that we take them with us. He doesn't know much about whaling; if you ask me, he's a fool."

Stubb laughed. "Well then, perhaps we could help you get rid of the whales," he said. "I'll come on board and have a little chat with your captain; would you mind translating?" asked Stubb.

The man smiled. "Not at all! I'd be very grateful if you could talk some sense into him."

The first mate lowered a rope ladder for Stubb to climb onto the ship. Then, he tapped lightly on the door of a nearby cabin. The door opened, and a small, delicate-looking man with a very large moustache emerged. He was wearing a fancy red velvet jacket with large gold buttons that glinted in the sun.

The first mate introduced Stubb to the captain and then started translating the conversation.

"Tell him," began Stubb, "that these two whales could cause his entire crew to become ill and die. The gases released by dead whales are poisonous and cause a fever for which there is no cure.

Explain to your captain that he has no choice but to free both whales immediately."

Of course, none of what Stubb was saying was true, and the first mate knew that he was lying. The captain, however, didn't realise that this was a trick and, as he listened to his first mate translate Stubb's words, a look of horror began to appear on his face.

The captain spoke quickly in French: "If that is the case, we must let the whales go immediately!"

Stubb nodded in agreement. "A wise move, sir. We could help you by dragging the smaller whale away from your boat if you like."

"Yes, yes, thank you," said the captain. "Thank you for your help, my good friend. You've saved the lives of my crew."

Stubb grinned. "Glad to be of service!" he said.

The two men shook hands and Stubb was accompanied back to his boat by the first mate. Then, the crew of the *Bouton de Rose* released the whale carcasses into the ocean. As promised, Stubb threw out a piece of rope and pretended to drag the smaller whale away.

Once the *Bouton de Rose* had disappeared into the distance, Stubb ordered us to row as close to the whale as possible.

I watched in amazement as Stubb picked up the boat-spade and began slicing into the whale at a point just behind the side-fin. He dug around inside the whale, much like a man digging for gold. The smell became progressively stronger and I feared that I might faint; I was about to beg Stubb to return to the ship, when he suddenly yelled: "I found it! I found it!"

The second mate placed his hands in the cavity and removed a spongy grey substance from the whale's stomach. Immediately, the horrible smell was replaced by a fragrance that reminded me of a garden of sweet-smelling roses.

"What is that?" I asked.

"It's ambergris, my boy," answered Stubb, his eyes sparkling. "Chemists use it to make the world's finest perfumes and it's worth a fortune. Those Frenchmen had no idea that they were carrying buried treasure!"

Stubb continued to greedily collect handfuls of ambergris while he explained that this valuable substance could only be found in the intestines of sick sperm whales. We would probably have spent

another hour there, in the middle of the ocean, collecting pieces of ambergris, had Ahab not appeared on deck and ordered Stubb to return to the ship immediately.

"You're wasting precious time, Stubb!" he cried. "Come back at once!"

"All right," said Stubb with a frown.

And so, we headed back to the *Pequod* to continue our pursuit of the whale, Moby Dick.

CHAPTER 7

SHORTLY AFTER OUR MEETING WITH THE *BOUTON DE ROSE*, WE crossed paths with the *Samuel Enderby*, an English ship from London. As soon as the ship was close enough, Ahab placed his hands around his mouth and shouted: "Ahoy there! Have you seen the white whale?"

He addressed the question to the captain of the ship, a strong, red-cheeked man of about sixty years of age, who was dressed in a flowing blue coat.

"Do you see this?" said the man, holding up his right arm. The arm looked as if it had been carved out of whalebone. "This is what that whale did to me."

Ahab's eyes widened in surprise. "The whale did that to you?"

The man nodded solemnly.

"He took my leg," said Ahab, pointing to his false leg.

The captain gave Ahab a sympathetic look. "Then we are both victims of the whale," he said.

"Tell me what happened to you," urged Ahab.

"Well," the captain began, "it happened a few years ago on my first journey along the equator. We had spotted about four or five whales, and had lowered the whaleboats to pursue them. I was about to harpoon one of the whales, when an enormous whale, with a wrinkled brow and milky-white head and hump, emerged from the water. He was the grandest whale I'd ever seen, and I decided to give chase. Unfortunately, the whale was cleverer than I had expected;

he disappeared underwater and, a second later, his huge tail came crashing down on our boat, splitting it in two. I was thrown into the sea, and one of the spears went through my arm. The wound was severe, and the doctor on board the ship feared that I would bleed to death. He had no choice but to remove my arm."

"And have you seen the whale since?" asked Ahab.

"Yes, twice," replied the captain. "The last time was a couple of weeks ago."

Ahab's eyes brightened. "Where? Where did you see him?"

The captain thought for a moment. "He was heading east, I think... You aren't planning to go after him, are you?"

"That is exactly what I am planning," said Ahab.

The captain frowned. "I suggest that you stay far away from that whale, no good can come from chasing Moby Dick, as you well know."

"I will hunt that whale for the rest of my days, if necessary," said Ahab. "He is like a magnet to me, I cannot resist pursuing him and I will not rest until he is dead... Thank you for the information, Captain."

Half an hour later, we had left the *Samuel Enderby* behind us, and were moving swiftly in an easterly direction.

***

The next day, we made an unfortunate discovery: some of the barrels containing the whale oil had started to leak. We had no choice but to stop sailing for a couple of days so that we could repair the barrels, and Starbuck volunteered to tell the captain the news. Initially, Ahab refused to stop the journey, but, realising that he could lose his men's trust, as well as the respect of the first mate, he finally agreed to drop anchor. The reason we had to stop sailing was because the barrels had to be brought up on deck to be repaired, and the extra weight could have caused the ship to become unbalanced and turn over.

At least one hundred barrels were removed from the hold over the next couple of days. Because he was one of the strongest men on board, Queequeg was given the task of passing the barrels to the other sailors on deck. He spent many hours walking barefoot in the dark, damp hold, and, as a result, ended up with a fever. For several days, Queequeg lay in a hammock, unable to eat or sleep. He

became frighteningly thin; his eyes bulged out of their sockets and his cheekbones poked through his cheeks.

One day, Queequeg made a very alarming request. "When somebody dies," he told me, "they put him in a long wooden box like a canoe." He meant a coffin, of course.

"On my island, when people die, they put them in a canoe and let it float out to sea. Please, tell the carpenter to make one of those canoes for me." He was convinced that he was close to death.

The rest of the crew protested; they believed that having a coffin on board would bring bad luck, but the carpenter felt obliged to do what had been asked of him, and he promptly took Queequeg's measurements.

When the coffin was ready, the carpenter brought it to Queequeg. The frail harpooner examined it from his hammock and nodded his approval.

"Now Ishmael, please bring me my harpoon and place it next to me. And bring a box of biscuits and a bottle of water," he asked. I did as I was told, though I had no idea what he intended to do with those items. With what little strength he had left, Queequeg lifted himself out of the hammock and lay down in the coffin. He crossed his arms on his chest, then asked me to do one more thing. "Bring Yojo," he said. Reluctantly, I did what was asked of me.

Queequeg fell asleep almost immediately, and I stayed nearby to comfort him and pray for him. But the harpooner did not need my comfort, or my prayers. Within a couple of days, my friend had made a miraculous recovery; the colour returned to his cheeks and his eyes sparkled as before.

"I cannot die yet, I still have much to do," he told me, as he climbed out of his coffin.

I stared at the harpooner in astonishment. "Do you really believe that a person can choose whether he will live or die?" I asked.

"If a man has made up his mind to live, illness cannot take him," said Queequeg.

I shook my head in disbelief and followed my friend below deck, where he proceeded to spend the afternoon sharpening his harpoon. And as for the coffin, it didn't go to waste; my friend used it as a sea chest to keep his things in.

CHAPTER 8

WE HAD NOT SEEN A WHALE IN WEEKS, AND OUR SPIRITS WERE understandably low. To make matters worse, we came across a ship called the *Bachelor* off the coast of Japan, which was on its way home to Nantucket, with hundreds of barrels of whale oil on board. The crew was clearly in a festive mood; they had tied colourful ribbons to the masts and were dancing to the beat of a drum on deck. We learned later that the crew of the *Bachelor* had enjoyed good fortune in Pacific waters; in fact they had killed so many whales that they had to convert pieces of wooden furniture into barrels to store the excess liquid.

As we passed the ship, our two captains had a brief conversation.

"Come aboard! Come aboard!" shouted the captain of the *Bachelor* to our very sad-looking Captain Ahab. "Come join the fun! We have plenty of food and drink, and plenty to celebrate!"

"Have you seen the white whale?" asked Ahab with a frown.

"No," replied the captain. "I've heard of him, but I don't believe he exists. Come celebrate with us!"

Ahab shook his head. "You are a full ship heading home, I am an empty ship heading out; it is best we continue on our journeys."

The captain of the *Bachelor* shrugged and we watched the ship glide across the water which shone in the afternoon sun. The sound of the drumbeat could be heard long after the ship had vanished, and I must confess to feeling quite jealous of the *Bachelor's* success, as well as a sudden longing to return home.

The *Bachelor's* good fortune seemed to help us, because, the next day, we managed to kill four whales; one whale for each harpoon boat. The whales were dragged to the ship, and we spent the evening celebrating our catch. After dinner, I went up on deck to enjoy the fresh night air. The moon had cast its silver light on the water and, as I stood at the railing, appreciating the stunning beauty of the scene in front of me, I heard muttering on the quarterdeck. I looked up and saw the captain and Fedallah talking.

"Have you had any more visions, Fedallah?" asked Ahab.

"I've had one," said the Persian. "It concerns your death…"

"What?" exclaimed Ahab. "What did you see? Will I die on this journey? Before my mission is complete?"

"I do not know for sure," the Persian replied. "All I know is that if it is your destiny to die on this voyage, I will die before you. And a rope will be the cause of your death."

"A rope?" said the captain. "Do you mean that I will be hanged? Impossible! I'm glad you told me this, Fedallah, now I know that I will kill Moby Dick and survive this journey. I am immortal at sea!"

With that, the two men walked away and I returned to the dining cabin, wishing I'd never heard that worrying conversation.

***

The blue skies and calm waters of the Pacific can often change and become dangerous. The region is known for its typhoons, which seem to burst unexpectedly out of a cloudless sky like exploding bombs. The following afternoon, we watched helplessly as the heavens filled with rolling dark clouds that threatened to bring destruction to the *Pequod*. The wind howled and raged about us, causing the ship to rock wildly from side to side. Loud thunder filled the air, and lightning lit up the blackened sky. The sight was both terrifying and impressive.

When a storm hits, the crew's first duty is to ensure that the harpoon boats are properly secured. I was in the middle of helping Starbuck and Stubb perform this task, when I heard some of the sailors cry out. They were pointing at the masts and shouting.

"The white lights! The white lights!" they cried.

I looked up, and to my amazement, saw three white flames rising from the masts.

"Have mercy on us all!" cried Stubb.

"Are the masts on fire?" I shouted to Starbuck. "Did the ship get struck by lightning?"

"No," he said. "Those lights have been known to appear during severe storms…they're considered to be a bad omen…"

"I never thought I'd live to see those lights!" said Stubb. "We're doomed! Doomed!"

Within minutes, the entire crew of the *Pequod* had gathered on deck. They watched the flames leap and dance above the masts with open mouths and disbelieving eyes.

"Aye, aye, men!" shouted Ahab, as he walked towards the quarterdeck. "Look at them! Those white flames are a sign! They light the way to the white whale! Nothing can stop us now, nothing! Not even a storm can keep us from destroying Moby Dick!"

Ahab threw his hands in the air and laughed maniacally. "This is our destiny!" he cried.

Burning with anger, Starbuck quickly climbed the steps that led to the quarterdeck and confronted his captain. "You're crazy, old man!" he shouted above the thunderous roar of the storm. "Don't you see? This storm is a warning… this mission of yours is cursed! You are putting us all in terrible danger! Let us adjust the sails and return home!"

"No!" cried Ahab. "We will continue our journey!" He turned to address the frightened crew below: "You took an oath to help me find the white whale… It is your duty to carry on till the very end, no matter what obstacles we may face! Return to your posts, at once!"

The men hurried off in various directions, too terrified to question the captain's authority.

Only Starbuck stayed where he was. "You'll regret this, old man! You won't be happy until you kill us all!"

Ahab glared at his first mate and walked away slowly.

CHAPTER 9

WITHIN TWO DAYS, THE TYPHOON HAD CALMED AND THE CREW of the *Pequod* could once again concentrate on the task of finding the white whale, Moby Dick. As we sailed through equatorial fishing waters, following the course that Ahab had planned, we came across a Nantucket whaling ship, the *Rachel*.

"Ahoy there!" shouted Ahab to the captain of the ship. "Have you seen the white whale?"

"Yes," confirmed the captain. "Have you by any chance seen a whaleboat?"

"No," answered Ahab.

The captain of the *Rachel* introduced himself as Captain Gardiner and asked Ahab for permission to board our ship; Ahab agreed.

"Tell me about the whale," said Ahab, when the two men were standing face to face. "When and where did you see him?"

"Late yesterday afternoon, about three miles south from here," replied Gardiner. "We had sent out three boats to hunt a school of whales, when we saw Moby Dick's white head and hump in the distance. We decided to send out a fourth boat to pursue the whale; the crew managed to harpoon him, but he pulled the boat with him for some distance… Night fell and the other three boats returned to the ship…" Gardiner paused. "We've searched everywhere for the fourth boat, but we can't find it. That's why I came on board, Captain, to ask for your help. Help us find the missing boat; I beg you, please help us!"

Ahab shook his head. "I can't do that, I'm afraid, we'll fall behind schedule if we stop now."

Gardiner looked at Ahab begging. "Please, Captain Ahab. My son was on that boat… he's only twelve years old! You must help me find him!"

Ahab sighed. "I said before, I cannot help you."

"But I'll pay you!" said Gardiner. "I'll pay you anything! Please!"

"I can't help you!" shouted Ahab. "Leave my ship at once!"

Gardiner stared at Ahab shocked. Avoiding the captain's look, Ahab walked quickly to his cabin and Gardiner was left with no

option but to return to his ship.

"We could've helped him find the lad," Stubb whispered to Starbuck.

"Aye," replied the first mate. "Ahab is letting his obsession turn him into a monster."

***

Shortly after the encounter with the *Rachel*, we crossed paths with another ship, the *Delight*. As the ship came closer, we noticed a shattered whaleboat tied to the quarter-deck. The dangling white planks and splinters of wood reminded me of a skeleton.

"Have you seen the white whale?" Ahab called out.

The captain of the *Delight* pointed to the wreckage and said, "Yes, and he did that."

"Did you kill him?" asked Ahab.

The captain shook his head. "No one can kill that whale."

Then, the captain of the *Delight* removed his hat and muttered a prayer, while his crew threw what appeared to be a body wrapped in fabric into the ocean.

"That whale killed six of my men," said the captain, by way of explanation. "We were only able to retrieve one body. I warn you, old man, stay away from Moby Dick."

Ahab ordered us to move on quickly, and we left the crew of the *Delight* to their misery.

The incident must have upset Ahab, because he spent the rest of the afternoon on deck, staring quietly into the ocean. At one moment, I saw a tear roll down his cheek and fall into the sea. Noticing the captain's distress, Starbuck walked up to Ahab and laid a hand on his shoulder.

The captain turned around quickly. "Oh, Starbuck," he said.

"Are you all right, Captain?" asked the mate.

"Oh, yes, yes, I'm fine," replied Ahab. "This day reminds me of the first time I killed a whale… I was just eighteen at the time. Do you know that I've been a whaling man for nearly forty years now? I've spent most of my life at sea, away from my wife, my son, my home in Nantucket… I have led a lonely life, Starbuck… I should be

home with my family; instead, I am here, chasing that wicked whale. This obsession is destroying me and I have grown tired of it…"

Starbuck looked relieved. "Then let us go home, Captain! Let us give up the search for the whale and return to our families safely."

Ahab sighed. "I wish I could do that," he said. "But something forces me to carry on searching for that evil creature. It is my destiny to kill Moby Dick and I cannot give up until I have succeeded in my quest…"

Disappointed by the captain's response, Starbuck simply shook his head and walked away.

Ahab continued to survey the sea, and was soon joined by Fedallah, who remained by his side until the sky was covered in stars.

CHAPTER 10

Later that night, Ahab, returned to his position on the quarterdeck. He had been there for about an hour when I noticed him sniffing the sea air. He scanned the dark water for several minutes before shouting: "There she blows! It's Moby Dick! There's his hump, as white as a snow-capped hill!"

A frenzy of activity followed: Starbuck was ordered to stay on board and steer the ship, while the three whaleboats belonging to Ahab, Flask and Stubb were dropped into the black ocean. Mates shouted instructions; oarsmen took up their positions and the chase began. All that was visible of the enormous whale was his hump, which resembled a large white island surrounded by bubbling sea foam.

Ahab's boat was the first to reach the whale and, sensing danger, the creature lifted his head out of the water. Then, he dived into the ocean and disappeared.

"He'll probably be down for at least an hour," Ahab muttered to Fedallah.

But the captain had underestimated Moby Dick's craftiness. The whale returned to the surface moments later with his enormous red mouth wide open, ready to devour Ahab's boat.

"Jump!" shouted the captain, as he caught sight of the whale's white teeth. Ahab and his crew had just seconds to dive out of harm's way before Moby Dick's powerful jaws grasped the little boat and crunched it into pieces. Satisfied with his victory, the whale swam away, leaving Ahab and his men to their fate.

The captain and his crew were rescued by the *Pequod* shortly afterwards. Once the other two boats had returned to the ship, Ahab summoned the crew on deck.

"Men," he began, "tonight the whale had his final triumph. Tomorrow, he will not be able to escape us. The doubloon is mine, because I was the first man to see the whale.

However, the first man who sees the whale on the day we succeed in killing him will receive the coin, and if I am the first man to see him, then I will give ten times the coin's worth to each and every man on this ship."

The men cheered, and many, including me, went to sleep. Ahab however, remained on deck until dawn, hoping to catch sight of his enemy, the white whale.

***

Shortly after noon the following day, one of the crew members, who was sitting in the crow's nest shouted: "There she blows! There she blows! The white whale, up ahead!"

Once again, three boats were lowered into the sea, while Starbuck stayed behind to man the ship. With Ahab's boat in the middle, the three whaleboats flew across the water in hot pursuit of the whale.

The boats approached Moby Dick directly and as soon as they were close enough, Ahab, Tashtego and Daggoo threw their harpoons into the animal's side. The whale twisted wildly in the water in a desperate effort to escape. He rolled over several times, causing the harpoon lines to become tangled. The quick-thinking Ahab grabbed a boat-knife and cut the line connecting his boat with the whale; but Flask and Stubb were not so fortunate. As a result of Moby Dick's furious wriggling, the two mates' boats crashed into each other, and both crews were thrown into the ocean.

Ahab and his men felt a sudden and violent impact, as Moby Dick smashed into their boat with his huge white forehead, sending it flying into the air. The boat turned over several times before landing

in the water, and Ahab and his crew were tossed into the sea.

Once again, the *Pequod* came to the rescue of its crew members, picking up sailors, planks and oars as it went. It was not until Ahab had been helped back on board the ship that the crew noticed that his false leg had been snapped off.

"Are you all right, Captain?" asked Stubb. "Did the whale injure you?"

"I'm fine," said Ahab. "The whale may have taken my leg, but I am still determined to destroy him." Ahab glanced around anxiously. "Is everyone here?"

The entire crew was present, except one man. The Persian was missing.

"Where is Fedallah?" asked Ahab anxiously. "Find him at once," he ordered. The crew searched every corner of the ship, but there was no trace of Fedallah.

"I'm sorry, sir," said Starbuck. "But he's not here."

"I think I saw him get tangled up in the lines," said Stubb. "He must have drowned."

Ahab was silent for a moment. "So, the first part of Fedallah's prophecy has come true. I can only hope that the rest of it does not… Prepare yourselves, men! Tomorrow, we will pursue Moby Dick for the last time; by evening that whale will be dead and we will be celebrating!"

Starbuck's jaw fell open. "You can't be serious!" he exclaimed. "That whale has destroyed four of our boats and killed a man; how can you expect us to keep risking our lives to capture him? Put an end to this madness, Ahab, I beg you!"

Ahab narrowed his eyes. "Do not question my authority, Starbuck. I have already explained to you that it is my destiny to destroy this whale. There is no other way. Men, prepare for the hunt; tomorrow, the whale is ours!"

And so, the crew members of the *Pequod* spent the whole night sharpening lances and harpoons and preparing the spare boats for the hunt. The carpenter was kept busy too, making a new leg for Ahab. The men worked in silence; only the sounds of hammers could be heard echoing through the night.

The third day of the hunt dawned, and crew members were ordered to stand at various points across the ship to keep looking for the whale.

"Do any of you see him?" Ahab shouted from the quarterdeck.

"No, sir, there's no sign of him," Starbuck replied.

"We must have passed him in the night," said Ahab. "Now the hunter has become the hunted… Turn the ship around, men!"

An hour or so later, the captain spotted Moby Dick's familiar white hump and cried out. "There he is! Lower the boats at once!"

The crew sprang into action, while Starbuck once again took command of the ship. The boats set out after the whale, but were met with an unexpected surprise when a group of sharks surfaced and began snapping hungrily at the oars.

"Keep rowing!" Ahab urged his sailors.

The whale disappeared under the water, but as Ahab and his men approached him, the huge white animal burst through to the surface, like an iceberg rising out of the ocean. The creature made a low threatening noise as he turned to face his pursuers.

"Keep going, men!" shouted Ahab.

The boats got closer to the whale, and the sailors could clearly see a number of harpoons and spears sticking out of his flesh.

"There!" yelled the captain. And then there was a sight that froze everyone. The white whale was carrying Fedallah's dead body tangled on its side!

Ahab was silent for a while. "I see him again," he finally whispered. "As he had said. Now my end must be near..."

"Attack, men!" he then shouted. Obviously angered by the attacks of the day before, the whale lifted its enormous tail and smashed Flask and Stubb's boats to pieces. Ahab's boat, however, was left untouched.

The whale sounded once more, and Ahab urged his crew to chase after him. Then, the sharks returned to resume their attack, biting and crunching the oars.

"The oars are getting smaller and smaller!" shouted a sailor.

"Never mind!" said Ahab. "Keep going!"

The whale drifted to the surface of the water, apparently unaware that Ahab's boat was nearby. Summoning up all his might, Ahab

threw his harpoon at the whale and watched it go through the creature's side. The whale's body jerked and bumped against the boat. Ahab and his crew managed to keep the boat steady, but one of the oarsmen was thrown into the ocean.

Then, Moby Dick prepared himself for his final act of destruction. He sped towards the *Pequod*, the source of all his troubles, and smashed his forehead into the ship, tearing a hole in the side of it.

"My ship!" yelled Ahab, as he watched the *Pequod* rapidly fill up with water.

The whale dived beneath the sinking ship, then surfaced once more a short distance from Ahab's boat.

"Die, you evil whale!" shouted the captain as he hurled his harpoon at the animal. The harpoon sank into Moby Dick's hump and the whale swam away quickly. Ahab tried to jump out of the way of the harpoon line, but it was too late. The rope caught Ahab by the throat, and dragged him into the water, much to the horror of his crew. But the greatest horror was yet to come: the sinking *Pequod* created a whirlpool in the middle of the ocean. Its force was so powerful that it pulled every single sailor down into the depths of the sea. The last picture of the *Pequod* was that of its three masts quickly sinking underwater with the ship's three harpooners perched on each one of them, as if they were still on the lookout for whales.

Within minutes, all traces of the *Pequod* had been eliminated. The whirlpool vanished, and the sea continued to roll on as it had for thousands of years.

I was the only man who survived Moby Dick's fury. When Fedallah died, Ahab chose me to replace him in his boat; I was thrown into the water when the whale bumped into it. By the time I reached the whirlpool, it had closed up. Fortunately, one souvenir of the Pequod remained: my friend Queequeg's coffin. As I approached the whirlpool, it shot out of the water and landed next to me. I climbed onto it, and waited. A whole day and night passed before the Rachel finally came to my rescue.

It saddens me when I think about the Pequod and all the friends I lost on that terrible day. But I learnt a valuable lesson on that journey: when a man becomes obsessed, he is certain to cause his own destruction and bring nothing but suffering to those closest to him.

Activity Section

CHAPTER 1

Comprehension

1 **Decide if the following sentences are True or False. Write T or F in the boxes.**

1. Ishmael arrived in New Bedford in order to take part in the whaling business. ☐

2. At first, Ishmael was afraid of Queequeg. ☐

3. Queequeg was collecting real human heads. ☐

4. When Ishmael jumped out of bed, the harpooner attacked him. ☐

5. Ishmael and Queequeg decided to go on a whaling trip together. ☐

2 **Choose a, b or c to complete the following sentences.**

1. Ishmael spent the night in New Bedford because
   a. he changed his mind about the trip.
   b. he had no money for the ferry.
   c. the ferry left without him.

2. Ishmael had to share a room with Queequeg because
   a. there were no rooms left in the inn.
   b. he couldn't afford a whole room.
   c. he wanted to meet the harpooner.

3. Queequeg had just returned from
   a. New Zealand.
   b. Rokovoko.
   c. Manhattan.

4. Queequeg reassured Ishmael that he wouldn't
   a. steal from him.
   b. make fun of him.
   c. hurt him.

5. Queequeg gave Ishmael
   a. all his belongings.
   b. a small wooden figure.
   c. half of his money.

Vocabulary

3 Complete the following sentences with the correct form of the words in the box.

| harpooners | grunt | blacksmith | landlord | pitch | light |

1. When I asked him about my wallet, he didn't answer, he just _____ behind his newspaper.
2. _____ use spears with long ropes in order to hunt whales.
3. It was _____ black in the cave and we didn't have a torch, so we couldn't see anything.
4. It is a comfortable, brightly _____ room with nice furniture and a big window.
5. The _____ made horseshoes out of iron.
6. Fortunately the _____ let them have the house at a low rent.

4 Find the words or phrases in Chapter 1 which mean the same as:

1. smiled widely _____ (page 6)
2. something you can pay for _____ (page 5)
3. the fat of sea animals _____ (page 4)
4. looking at something or someone for a long time _____ (page 5)
5. a group of people with the same race, beliefs and language _____ (page 10)
6. everything a man has in his possession _____ (page 11)
7. ate hungrily without properly chewing the food _____ (page 6)
8. without really wanting to _____ (page 6)

Follow-up activities

5 Discuss.

1. What do you think are the advantages and disadvantages of going on a whaling trip? Would you be able to spend time at sea?
2. What do you know about whaling? How popular is it today?
3. Would you ever share a room with a stranger if you had to?
4. Whales are large sea animals which are endangered. What other endangered species do you know of? Why is it important to protect them?
5. Do you think that the harpooner is a trustworthy person after all? What do you think will happen next?

6 Imagine that you are Peter Coffin, the owner of the inn. Write a page in your diary about Ishmael's first night at the inn and his meeting with Queequeg. (120-140 words)

CHAPTER 2

Comprehension

1 **Read Chapter 2 and match the two halves of the sentences.**

1. Ishmael chose
2. Peleg and Bilald
3. Captain Ahab's leg
4. A stranger warned the two friends
5. Ishmael and Queequeg

a. was eaten by a whale.
b. the *Pequod* for the voyage.
c. boarded the ship on Christmas Day.
d. were the owners of the ship.
e. that Captain Ahab was a dangerous man.

2 **Complete the summary of Chapter 2 using words or short phrases.**

Queequeg suggested that Ishmael should choose (**1**)_____ for their trip. So, Ishmael went to the harbour and after some searching he decided that (**2**)_____was suitable for them. He talked to one of the (**3**) _____ of the ship, Peleg, who warned him against the dangers of a whaling trip. Peleg also informed him that Captain Ahab had (**4**) _____ to a whale. However, Ishmael was still (**5**) _____ to join the crew. The next day Queequeg and Ishmael went to the ship and signed the relevant papers. As they were leaving, they (**6**) _____ a strange man. He told them that Captain Ahab was a (**7**) _____ and (**8**)_____ person. Despite the warnings, the two friends boarded the ship on Christmas Day.

Vocabulary

3 **Find the words or phrases in Chapter 2 which mean the same as:**

1. white bone that comes from an elephant's tusks   i _____ (page 12)
2. angry and violent   f _____ (page 12)
3. the people who work on a ship   c _____ (page 14)
4. very willing to do sth   e _____ (page 14)
5. make sth sound very important   e _____ (page 14)
6. to begin a journey   s _____ (page 18)

4 Complete the following sentences using the words in the box.

deck	ran into	polish	negotiate	fog	supplies

1. Yesterday I _____ an old classmate of mine. He hadn't changed at all!
2. The _____ in our area makes driving conditions really dangerous.
3. Did you _____ your shoes?
4. Before we leave on our camping trip, we need to buy all the necessary _____ .
5. They tried to _____ the price but the salesman insisted that the car cost €15,000.
6. He went up to the _____ to enjoy the view of the islands at sunset.

Follow-up activities

5 Discuss.

1. Do you think a person should trust his/her instincts in order to make decisions?
2. A man warned Ishmael and Queequeg that Captain Ahab was obsessed with the whale that took his leg. What do you think that means? Why does the man say that Ahab's obsession has driven him mad?
3. Ishmael was not discouraged by Peleg's warnings against whaling. If you were in his position would you give it a second thought? Do you believe it is worth taking risks in life?
4. Do you think that the strange man and his warnings can be seen as a sign for the *Pequod's* voyage?
5. Ishmael saw five dark figures on the deck. Who do you think these people were? Could they be dangerous?

6 Imagine that you are Peleg and you need to tell Bildad about Ishmael. How would you describe him?
(120-140 words)

CHAPTER 3

Comprehension

1 **Read the following statements. In each box write T if the sentence is True and F if it is False.**

1. Each mate was responsible for two whaleboats. ☐
2. Ishmael admired Captain Ahab for his courage. ☐
3. Captain Ahab gathered the crew in order to make an announcement. ☐
4. Captain Ahab wanted to kill Moby Dick for its oil. ☐
5. Starbuck did not agree with Captain Ahab. ☐
6. There was a reward for the person who spotted Moby Dick first. ☐

2 **Read chapter 3 and match the two halves of the sentences.**

1. One morning Captain Ahab
2. Moby Dick
3. Captain Ahab
4. Ishmael
5. After the announcement

a. ruined Captain Ahab's life.
b. wanted to take revenge on the white whale.
c. asked the crew to assemble on the deck.
d. there was a celebration.
e. wanted to learn more about the incident with the whale.

Vocabulary

3 **Choose a, b or c to complete the following sentences.**

1. Can you _____ the difference between the two pictures?
   a. spot   **b.** pinch   **c.** blaze
2. My father felt great _____ after he lost his fortune.
   a. sympathy   **b.** row   **c.** sorrow
3. She had a terrible _____ when she heard the unexpected news.
   a. fit   **b.** cheekbone   **c.** suffering
4. All the students must _____ in the library before lunch time.
   a. survey   **b.** assemble   **c.** trigger

5. He is attractive although he has a _____ nose.

   a. wrinkled   **b.** stout   **c.** crooked

6. The accident left a _____ on Harry's left leg.

   a. hammer   **b.** scar   **c.** nail

4   **Complete the following sentences with the correct from of the words in capitals.**

1. Sheila was filled with_____for her sister and wanted to be just like her.   **ADMIRE**

2. Lorrie paced _____ outside the doctor's office as she waited for her turn to come.   **PATIENCE**

3. His actions prove that he is a _____ person.   **COURAGE**

4. Financial matters are the company's _____ now.   **PRIOR**

Follow-up activities

5   **Discuss.**

1. If you were a member of the *Pequod's* crew would you agree with Captain Ahab's obsession or not?

2. What do you think about Captain Ahab's personality? Do you feel admiration for him or do you have different feelings? Do you think his rage is justified?

3. Do you think there is any point in taking revenge, especially on an animal?

4. Starbuck doesn't seem to share his captain's feelings or plans. Do you think he is right or wrong to do so?

5. Do you think it will be easy for the men on the *Pequod* to find the white whale? Do you think Captain Ahab's plan will be helpful in this quest?

6   **Imagine that you are Captain Ahab, describe how you lost your leg and how you feel about Moby Dick. Describe in detail your feelings and your intentions towards him.**
(120-140 words)

CHAPTER 4

Comprehension

1 **Answer the following questions.**

1. What happened a week after the celebrations?

_____

2. Who was Fedallah?

_____

3. Was the men's first attempt to catch a whale successful?

_____

4. How did they survive in the Cape of Good Hope?

_____

5. What did Starbuck think of the giant squid?

_____

2 **Complete the sentences with the correct word(s).**

1. Ahab gave orders to the _____ dressed in black.

2. _____ is when whales stay underwater, sometimes for a long time.

3. According to a rumour, Fedallah could _____.

4. As the *Pequod* was sailing towards _____, Dagoo spotted _____ .

5. Queequeg believed that when one sees a _____, it means that he will probably catch a _____ soon after.

Vocabulary

3 **Choose the correct word to complete the sentences.**

1. The boat was **floating/rowing** out to sea.

2. The research **encounters/indicates** a rise in criminality.

3. The fireman managed to **sink/rescue** the child from the burning building.

4. To Laura's **astonishment/rumour** no one came to the party.

5. Mario did not answer my question, he just **dropped/shrugged** his shoulders and left.

6. We have to do as the leader **commands/chains**.

4 **Complete the crossword with words from Chapter 4.**

1. Long, thin arms of several creatures, such as octopus or squid
2. A pole with a sharp point at one end, sometimes used as a weapon
3. A piece of thick cord made of strings of cotton
4. To move and send out air
5. A sea creature with 10 short arms and a long soft body
6. What is extracted from the whale
7. To speak very quietly

Follow-up activities

5 **Discuss.**

1. Peleg and Bildad told Ahab not to take part in any whale hunt because of his leg. But he brought his own crew in order to command his own whaleboat. What does this show about his character?
2. Why do you think the first attempt to catch a whale was unsuccessful? Do you think that Ishmael and Queequeg felt disappointed?
3. How do you think Queequeg and Ishmael felt when they were tossed into the water? How would you react if you were in their position? Would you panic?
4. Do you believe Fedallah is a good or a bad person? They say he has the ability to see the future. Do you believe a person can predict the future or not?
5. The business of extracting the oil will be described in the next Chapter. How do you think this is done?

6 **Imagine you are Ishmael and write a letter to your family about your first attempt to catch a whale. Explain how you felt when the boat broke, you fell into the water and stayed there for a long time. (120-140 words)**

CHAPTER 5

Comprehension

1 **Read the questions and choose the correct answer.**

1. What is the initial phase of fat removal called?
   a. cutting-in
   b. spermaceti

2. Where does spermaceti come from?
   a. a whale's head
   b. a whale's carcass

3. Where was the oil put?
   a. Below the deck into a room.
   b. Into barrels.

4. Who was chosen to get the liquid out of the whale's head?
   a. Queequeg
   b. Tashtego

5. Why did Tashtego fall?
   a. He slipped.
   b. Someone pushed him.

6. Who saved Tashtego?
   a. Dagoo
   b. Queequeg

2 **Put the following events in the order which they happened. Write 1-7 in the boxes.**

a. The blubber was cut into strips and then boiled in the try-pots. ☐

b. Tashtego spent two hours removing the spermaceti. ☐

c. Queequeg dived off the ship and saved Tashtego. ☐

d. The whale was lifted out of the water and a hook was inserted into its flesh. ☐

e. The harpooner slipped and fell into the whale's head. ☐

f. Starbuck chose Tashtego to extract the spermaceti from the whale's head. ☐

g. The blubber was removed from the whale's body. ☐

Vocabulary

3 Complete the following sentences using the correct form of the words in the box.

| hook | carry out | vanish | boil | bucket | slip |

1. Five _____ of water weren't enough for our thirsty plants.
2. Isn't this _____ big for that kind of fish?
3. Some _____ oil fell on his leg and he was taken to hospital.
4. He _____ into the dark; we never saw him again.
5. Our grandma _____ and broke her arm.
6. This is a difficult mission to _____.

4 What do the following phrases from Chapter 5 mean? Choose the correct option and match 1-8 with a-h.

1. carcass
2. roll
3. frothy
4. peel
5. sway
6. precious
7. railing
8. mast

a. to remove the skin of fruit and vegetables
b. the body of a dead animal
c. one of a set of rails making a fence
d. valuable
e. full of a mass of white bubbles
f. to move slowly from side to side
g. to move by turning over and over
h. a tall pole that supports the sails on a ship

Follow-up activities

5 Discuss.

1. Do you think killing an animal is always cruel or do you believe that sometimes this is a natural process that needs to be done?
2. Queequeg did not hesitate to dive into the water and save Tashtego. What does this show about him? Would you have done the same?
3. Queequeg says to Ishmael: "you can achieve just about anything if you have enough faith and courage". Do you agree or not? What else may be needed?
4. What do you think is more important or necessary for people: the whale's blubber or its spermaceti? Why?
5. Do you think that the *Pequod's* men will have more luck with whales?

6 You are Captain Ahab. Write a report of the process of fat removal from the whale for Peleg and Bildad. (120-140 words)

CHAPTER 6

Comprehension

1 **Read Chapter 6 and match the two halves of the sentences.**

1. Ishmael and Queequeg
2. *Bouton de Rose*
3. Two dead whales
4. Stubb
5. Chemists

a. use ambergris to make fine perfumes.
b. were attached to the French ship.
c. noticed a heavy smell as they were passing their time.
d. was the name of a French ship that came near the *Pequod*.
e. convinced the French captain to give him the carcasses.

2 **Find words/phrases spoken by the characters in Chapter 6 which:**

1. Stubb uses to refer to the dead whales of the other ship (page 38)

_____

2. show the *Bouton de Rose's* first mate's opinion of his captain (page 38)

_____

3. show the *Bouton de Rose's* captain's reaction to Stubb's words (page 40)

_____

4. show the value of ambergris (page 40)

_____

Vocabulary

3 **Choose a, b or c to complete the following sentences.**

1. When I broke the window, both my parents looked at me with a _____.
   a. frown   **b.** mat   **c.** light
2. When you meet someone for the first time it's nice to _____ hands.
   a. shield   **b.** dig   **c.** shake
3. The lion _____ the little animal under a tree to eat it.
   a. dragged   **b.** weaved   **c.** accompanied

4. Tom and Julia asked Lucy if she would join them and she _____.

   a. failed   **b.** nodded   **c.** realised

5. Where is this strong _____ coming from?

   a. mission   **b.** rosebud   **c.** odour

6. There were _____ flying above their heads.

   a. cavities   **b.** vultures   **c.** substances

4   Complete the following sentences using words from Chapter 6.

1. Unfortunately, there is no c_____ for this disease yet.

2. Talk some s_____ into your son, he's got expelled from school again!

3. Stop eating so g_____, you'll have trouble with your stomach!

4. Dean was reading an article about people's p_____ of happiness.

5. Sue is so bossy, she always o_____ people around.

Follow-up activities

5   Discuss.

1. "Life at sea can be very lonely," reads the text. Do you agree? Why?/Why not?

2. Ishmael wanted to join Stubb on his mission. Why do you think he insisted?

3. Stubb lied to the French captain to get what he wanted. Do you agree with that? Would you have done the same? Do you think there are innocent lies?

4. Ahab said to Stubb that he was wasting time. Why wasn't he interested in ambergris?

5. Do you think the *Pequod* and its crew are closer to Moby Dick now?

6   Imagine you are the French captain. Write a letter to your family, telling them all about the dead whales. Explain why you believe that you were saved by Stubb. (120-140 words)

CHAPTER 7

Comprehension

1 **Answer the following questions.**

1. What had happened to the captain of the *Samuel Enderby*?

_____

2. Why did the *Pequod* stop sailing for a couple of days?

_____

3. How did Queequeg get sick?

_____

4. Why did Queequeg ask for a coffin?

_____

2 **Complete the sentences with the correct names from the box.**

Ahab	Ishmael	Queequeg	Starbuck

1. _____ met a captain who was Moby Dick's victim as well.
2. _____ had to tell Captain Ahab some bad news.
3. _____ was transferring the barrels to the deck because he was very strong.
4. _____ asked for his harpoon and _____ brought it to him.
5. _____ couldn't eat anything and he lost a lot of weight.

Vocabulary

3 **Find the words or phrases in Chapter 7 which mean the same as:**

1. to lose so much blood that your
   life is at risk   _____ (page 44)
2. to get out through a hole   _____ (page 44)
3. to stay in a flat position   _____ (page 44)
4. to stop sailing   _____ (page 44)
5. cannot do otherwise   _____ (page 44)
6. to decide to do something   _____ (page 46)
7. when one gets better from an illness _____ (page 46)

80

4 **Complete the following sentences with the correct form of the words in capitals.**

1. The building was an _____ choice of place
   for the event; we'll be more careful next time!   FORTUNATE
2. She hopes that her _____ will be
   answered some day.   PRAY
3. The teacher gave them a _____ smile
   and the students realised he would be on their side.   SYMPATHY
4. After so many efforts the patient seems to have lost
   all his _____ .   STRONG
5. His mother looked at him in _____ as
   it was obvious that he was lying.   BELIEVE
6. You need your parents' _____ to
   participate in the field trip.   APPROVE
7. We need to take the _____ of the room
   for the carpet.   MEASURE

Follow-up activities

5 **Discuss.**

1. Does the captain of the *Samuel Enderby* want to take revenge on Moby Dick? Do you think that he is a coward or simply a realistic person? Why / Why not?
2. At first when they discovered the leak, Ahab refused to stop the trip. What do you think of this reaction? Do you believe that his obsession could be dangerous?
3. Why did Queequeg order a coffin? How do you think he was feeling? What is strange about his request?
4. How did Queequeg recover? Do you think that he was seriously ill or not? Have you ever recovered so quickly from an illness?
5. What do you think Captain Ahab will do after the repairs on the ship are finished?

6 **"If a man has made up his mind to live, illness cannot take him." Discuss these words. Do you believe that the power of the mind affects our body? (120-140 words)**

CHAPTER 8

Comprehension

1 **Read the following statements and decide if they are True or False. Write T or F in the boxes.**

1. The *Bachelor* didn't have much whale oil.
2. Fedallah had a strange dream about Ahab's death.
3. They were sailing in the Pacific when a severe storm broke out.
4. During the storm Ishmael was helping Starbuck and Stubb to check the boats.
5. The *Pequod* was hit by lightning.
6. Ahab wanted to stop the journey because of the white lights.

2 **Match the two halves of the sentences.**

1. The *Bachelor*
2. Fedallah
3. The captain of the *Bachelor*
4. Starbuck
5. The crew

a. made a prediction about Ahab's death.
b. obeyed their captain because they were afraid of him.
c. brought the *Pequod* good luck.
d. invited everybody on board to celebrate.
e. got very angry with Ahab.

Vocabulary

3 **Complete the sentences with the appropriate word from Chapter 8.**

1. I must c_____ that I'm responsible for what happened.
2. She had a v_____ in which an angel appeared before her.
3. A lot of people believe that a black cat is a bad o_____.
4. Their father looked at them sternly and m_____ something between his teeth.
5. I don't believe in d_____, people make their own fate.

4 Do the crossword.

1. Very short in time
2. One who never dies
3. A strong desire
4. Bad weather with strong wind, rain, lightning and thunder
5. To make a loud noise
6. A violent tropical storm
7. A bright stream of burning gas that comes from something that is on fire

Follow-up activities

5 Discuss.

1. Have you ever experienced a storm? What other types of extreme weather do you know of? What is usual for your country?
2. Fedallah had a strange vision. Can you guess what his vision means? Will it come true? What do you believe will happen?
3. Ahab doesn't seem to believe Fedallah's vision. He says that he's immortal at sea. What does this show about his character? Do you think that he is arrogant?
4. Do you agree with Starbuck's anger? If you were a member of the crew how would you react to Ahab's insistence?
5. Do you think that Starbuck and Ahab will make up or stay angry with each other?

6 Imagine that you are Starbuck. Write a letter to your family telling them what happened on the day of the storm and why you got so angry with Captain Ahab. Explain how you felt and what you thought about the captain's obsession. (120-140 words)

CHAPTER 9

Comprehension

1 **Complete the following sentences by choosing a, b or c.**

1. Captain Gardiner
   a. had lost one whaling boat.
   b. had managed to harpoon Moby Dick.
   c. had lost three whaling boats.
2. Ahab refused to
   a. talk to Gardiner.
   b. help Gardiner.
   c. let Gardiner board his ship.
3. The captain of the *Delight*
   a. had lost six of his men to the whale.
   b. wanted to kill Moby Dick.
   c. was looking for his son.
4. Ahab
   a. killed his first whale when he was forty years old.
   b. had had a very lonely life.
   c. hadn't seen his family for eighteen years.
5. Starbuck
   a. tried to help Gardiner.
   b. wasn't worried about Ahab.
   c. asked Ahab to let them all return home.

2 **What do the words in bold type refer to?**

1. "When and where did you see **him**?" (page 52)

2. "I can't do **that**, I'm afraid, …" (page 52)

3. "We could've helped him find the **lad**," (page 54)

4. "Yes, and he did **that**." (page 54)

5. "…and I've grown tired of **it**…" (page 56)

6. "I wish I could do **that**," (page 56)

Vocabulary

3 **Complete the following sentences using the correct preposition in the box.**

by	into	on	out	across

1. The new members of the crew came _____ board yesterday.
2. The ship sent _____ an SOS.
3. Unfortunately he fell _____ their trap.
4. We came _____ an old friend we hadn't seen for years.
5. The students need to carry _____ working hard.
6. Who's calling _____ 'help'?
7. Have you _____ any chance seen my wallet?

4 **Choose the correct word to complete the sentences.**

1. When Alan heard the good news he **sighed/noticed** with relief.
2. Instead of saying no, Barbara **shook/muttered** her head.
3. The film is about the **response/quest** for gold in California of the 19th century.
4. You can't **force/retrieve** me to follow you, I don't want to go camping.
5. Martha's **looked/grown** tired of her daughter's immature behaviour.
6. The **wreckage/splinters** of the aircraft was a shocking sight.

Follow-up activities

5 **Discuss.**

1. Why do you think Ahab refused to help Gardiner find the missing whaleboat? How do you judge his decision? What would you have done in his position?
2. Ahab has been a whaling man for nearly forty years now. How do you think he is dealing with his loneliness? What can make someone choose a profession like that?
3. Starbuck says that Ahab's obsession has turned him into a monster. Do you agree with this? Is it too late for Ahab to change?
4. Do you believe in destiny? Can people always use their free will to do anything they want?
5. Do you think that Ahab will succeed in his quest?

6 **Write an essay about obsessions and how people should deal with them. Give examples of various obsessions and explain how they affect everyday life and people's mentality and character. (120-140 words)**

CHAPTER 10

Comprehension

1 **Answer the questions.**

1. How many times did the crew face Moby Dick?

_____

2. How many boats were lowered into the sea each time?

_____

3. Did Fedallah's prophecy come true? What happened to Fedallah?

_____

4. What happened to Ahab in the end?

_____

5. Who was the only survivor and how did he survive?

_____

2 **Match the two halves of the sentences.**

1. Starbuck
2. Fedallah
3. After the first attack
4. Ishmael
5. Dagoo, Tashtego and Queequeg
6. Ahab
7. Moby Dick

a. got tangled in the ropes around the whale and drowned.
b. destroyed Ahab's leg once more.
c. asked Ahab to stop this madness.
d. the captain said the doubloon was his.
e. was saved by the *Rachel*.
f. went down with the ship.
g. died by his own harpoon line.

Vocabulary

3 **Complete the sentences using the words in the box.**

| steered | sense | cheering | tangled | jaw | jerk |

1. Although we barely know each other, I _____ that he is not a good person.

2. The boys realised something was wrong when the car stopped with a _____.

3. The captain _____ the boat towards the coast.

4. Crocodiles can't move their upper _____.

5. Alison never puts any makeup on and always has _____ hair.

6. The crowd was _____ when the famous band entered the stage.

4 **Complete the sentences with the correct form of the words in capitals.**

1. My grandfather always gave me _____ advice.   VALUE

2. Tom likes cheating people, he is famous for his _____.   CRAFT

3. The children finished their homework _____ in order to watch their favourite TV series.   RAPID

4. After the burglary a lot of things were missing, but the jewellery had remained _____.   TOUCH

5. All students will be punished, _____ the headmaster's son.   INCLUDE

6. The volcano Vesuvius was responsible for the _____ of Pompei.   DESTROY

Follow-up activities

5 **Discuss.**

1. Starbuck complains but he doesn't really take command of the situation. If you were in his position would you have tried to find more decisive ways to stop Captain Ahab?

2. Ahab is missing a long time from home and in the end he dies at sea. If you were a member of Ahab's family how would you feel? Do you think being away from your family is painful?

3. Have you ever got obsessed with a certain goal in your life? If you don't achieve a goal do you get disappointed? Do you believe that setting unrealistic goals can lead us to madness or depression?

4. Ishmael says that he was taught an important lesson. Do you agree with him? What did you get from this story?

6 **Imagine you are a newspaper reporter. Write an article under the following headline: 'The white whale strikes again - the *Pequod's* sole survivor escapes Moby Dick on a coffin!' (120-140 words)**

Moby Dick
Student's Book
by Herman Melville adapted by H.Q. Mitchell

Published by: **MM Publications**

www.mmpublications.com

info@mmpublications.com

Offices
UK Cyprus France Greece Poland Turkey USA
Associated companies and representatives throughout the world.

Produced in the EU

ISBN: 978-960-478-004-4   C1212006032-7154